Grandmothers

by Lola M. Schaefer

Consulting Editor: Gail Saunders-Smith, Ph.D.

Consultant: Phyllis Edelbrock, First-Grade Teacher,
University Place School District, Washington

Pebble Books

an imprint of Capstone Press
Mankato, Minnesota

Pebble Books are published by Capstone Press
818 North Willow Street, Mankato, Minnesota 56001
http://www.capstone-press.com

Library of Congress Cataloging-in-Publication Data
Schaefer, Lola M., 1950–
    Grandmothers/by Lola M. Schaefer.
    p. cm.—(Families)
    Includes bibliographical references and index.
    Summary: Simple text and photographs depict grandmothers, where they go,
and what they do.
    ISBN 0-7368-0258-4
    1. Grandmothers—Juvenile literature. 2. Grandmothers—Pictorial works—
Juvenile literature. [1. Grandmothers.] I. Title. II. Series: Schaefer, Lola M., 1950–
Families.
HQ759.9.S35   1999
306.874′5—dc21   98-45156
                                                                                 CIP
                                                                                  AC

Note to Parents and Teachers

The Families series supports national social studies standards for
units related to identifying family members and their roles in the
family. This book describes and illustrates grandmothers and
activities they do with their grandchildren. The photographs
support emergent readers in understanding the text. The repetition
of words and phrases helps emergent readers learn new words.
This book also introduces emergent readers to subject-specific
vocabulary words, which are defined in the Words to Know section.
Emergent readers may need assistance to read some words and to
use the Table of Contents, Words to Know, Read More, Internet
Sites, and Index/Word List sections of the book.

2

Table of Contents

Grandmothers are mothers of fathers or mothers.

This grandmother
plays basketball.

This grandmother
visits a library.

This grandmother
plays at a park.

This grandmother works
at a garden store.

This grandmother
cheers at a game.

This grandmother paints.

This grandmother
ties shoes.

This grandmother blows
a kiss to her grandchild.

Words to Know

basketball—a game played on a court by two teams; players score by throwing a ball through a high net.

grandchild—the child of a person's son or daughter

grandmother—the mother of a person's mother or father

library—a place people go to read or borrow books, magazines, newspapers, tapes, and videos

visit—to go to see people or places away from home

Read More

Bailey, Debbie. *Grandma.* Toronto: Annick Press, 1994.

Do Mommies Have Mommies?: First Questions and Answers about Families. Library of First Questions and Answers. Alexandria, Va.: Time-Life for Children, 1994.

Saunders-Smith, Gail. *Families.* People. Mankato, Minn.: Pebble Books, 1998.

Internet Sites

Grandma's Room
http://www.grandmama.com

National Grandparents Day
http://www.grandparents-day.com

Treasure Maps in Genealogy Research
http://www.firstct.com/fv/tmaps.html

Index/Word List

basketball, 7
blows, 21
cheers, 15
fathers, 5
game, 15
garden, 13
grandchild, 21
kiss, 21
library, 9

mothers, 5
paints, 17
park, 11
plays, 7, 11
shoes, 19
store, 13
ties, 19
visits, 9
works, 13

Word Count: 50
Early-Intervention Level: 5

Editorial Credits

Mari C. Schuh, editor; Steve Weil/Tandem Design, cover designer and illustrator;
Kimberly Danger, photo researcher

Photo Credits

International Stock/Scott Barrow, 4
Mark Turner, cover, 6, 8, 12, 14, 16, 18, 20
PhotoBank, Inc., 1; PhotoBank, Inc./Lew Lause, 10

Special thanks to Joy Allison, Lori Hollenback, and Penny McCarthy, first-grade
teachers at Evergreen Primary in University Place, Washington, for reviewing the
books in the Families series.